PRACTICAL STUFF FOR PASTORS

LEADING
CHANGE

Loveland, CO

Group

Real. **Bold.** Love.

Group resources actually work!

This Group resource incorporates our R.E.A.L. approach to ministry. It reinforces a growing friendship with Jesus, encourages long-term learning, and results in life transformation, because it's

Relational
Learner-to-learner interaction enhances learning and builds Christian friendships.

Experiential
What learners experience through discussion and action sticks with them up to 9 times longer than what they simply hear or read.

Applicable
The aim of Christian education is to equip learners to be both hearers and doers of God's Word.

Learner-based
Learners understand and retain more when the learning process takes into consideration how they learn best.

PRACTICAL STUFF FOR PASTORS:
LEADING CHANGE

Credits
Editor: Rick Edwards
Assistant Editors: Kelsey Perry, Ardeth Carlson
Art and Design: Amy Taylor, Andy Towler, Darrin Stoll
Contributing Authors: Shirley Giles Davis, Susan Lawrence, Austin Maxheimer, Tony Myles, Josh Schuler, Brian Walton

Unless otherwise indicated, all Scripture quotations are taken from the *Holy Bible*, New Living Translation, copyright © 1996, 2004, 2007, 2013 by Tyndale House Foundation. Used by permission of Tyndale House Publishers, Inc., Carol Stream, Illinois 60188. All rights reserved.

ISBN 978-1-4707-2325-5

Printed in the United States of America.

10 9 8 7 6 5 4 3 2 1   24 23 22 21 20 19 18 17 16 15

CONTENTS

INTRODUCTION

When we at Group Publishing wondered what kind of resource we could offer to pastors, we asked hundreds of pastors what they wish they'd learned in seminary, but didn't. The overwhelming response was "practical stuff." This book is our response.

However, if you need fix the faucet in the first floor ladies' room, Google it. This book isn't *that* practical.

If you want to know the best accounting practices to prepare for an IRS audit of a 501(c)(3) nonprofit religious organization, consult a tax lawyer. We didn't have enough pages to cover such a complicated subject.

And if you are looking for the perfect volume setting on the sanctuary sound system that satisfies everyone...well, we all know that book will never be written.

Practical Stuff for Pastors is a series of handbooks dedicated to topics such as how to manage a team, handle property and financial issues, diffuse conflicts, lead change, and more. We've assembled a team of pastors, church leaders, and business professionals who provide tips, recommendations, and strategies for the practical responsibilities pastors deal with on a regular basis.

In keeping with this book's practical approach, you'll find that the table of contents doubles as a topical index. The plain, straightforward chapter titles don't try to be clever but clearly describe the topic they address. The stand-alone chapters can be read in any sequence, at any time you need to access them. The writing style is informal, with easy, accessible language. (And we used mostly short words!)

So whenever you need to look up how to do some practical ministry stuff:

1. Look up your topic in the table of contents.
2. Read the chapter.
3. Act on what you read: make a call, plan a meeting, create a job description, or delegate a task.

Leading Change

This volume of Practical Stuff for Pastors focuses on how to lead the process of change in a local church.

If ever there was an organization that resists change, it would be the church. Reliance on tradition, whether decades or centuries old, is part of our DNA. And for good reason: Who wants to rehash the nature and relationships of the Divine Trinity? Who is up for re-establishing the biblical canon every five years? Creeds and actions that have deep roots in the church's worship and practice continue to feed and guide Christians today.

And yet, another part of our DNA includes the impulse to change. Church history is replete with reform movements, big and small. Perhaps you've heard of St. Benedict or St. Francis, Martin Luther, John Wesley, or Martin Luther King, Jr. If these names don't ring a bell, surely you will recognize the words of St. Paul of Tarsus: "Anyone who belongs to Christ has become a new person. The old life is gone; a new life has begun! And all of this is a gift from God, who brought us back to himself through Christ" (2 Corinthians 5:17-18).

The transformation of the individual in Christ has far-reaching implications. People who have experienced the life-changing grace of God should know how important positive change can be. But wait, there's more…change in God's world isn't limited to individual persons. God aims to change our world, even the entire cosmos:

> "But forget all [the past]—it is nothing compared to what I am going to do. For I am about to do something new. See, I have already begun! Do you not see it?" (Isaiah 43:18-19)

> "Then I saw a new heaven and a new earth, for the old heaven and the old earth had disappeared… And the one sitting on the throne said, 'Look, I am making everything new!'" (Revelation 21:1, 5)

The greatest news of all is that God invites us to participate in this change process! May this handbook be a small help as you lead change in your arena of God's cosmic change movement.

VISION: THE FOUNDATION OF CHANGE

Sarah couldn't put her finger on it, but she knew something was wrong in her church. "It just feels like something is missing," she shared with her friend Adam. The Sunday services were...fine. The sermons were biblical, the music was good, and the prayers seemed genuine. There really wasn't anything wrong with the church, and yet they were slowly losing members and had been for quite some time. "It's not like a mass exodus or anything," she explained. "We're just losing a few families every year. I'm not sure that most people have even noticed." Adam was sympathetic, but he didn't know how to relate to what she was feeling, as his experience with his church was entirely different. Finally, he invited Sarah to visit his church the following Sunday, "Maybe it will help you figure out what's missing at your church." Sarah agreed.

When she visited Adam's church, Sarah was overwhelmed. There was a nearly palpable energy and enthusiasm among the people. She read in the bulletin their stated vision to see people use the one life they've been given to impact others for Jesus. A number of reports on current community ministry projects were also printed. In the service, she heard a testimony from someone who had recently served at the local crisis pregnancy center. During the sermon, the pastor shared several more stories of community impact. He followed it up with a gentle reminder from James 4:14 that our lives "are like a morning fog—it's here a little while, then it's gone" and passionately challenged everyone to make their lives truly count.

This visit highlighted the invisible problem with Sarah's church. Her pastor and church lacked a clear, compelling vision, and thus drifted, over time, to an inward focus.

Any book about leading change must begin with a discussion about vision because efforts to introduce change into a church should be made within the context of a compelling, overarching vision. George Barna describes vision as "a clear mental image of a preferable future."[1] Leaders must have in their minds and on their hearts a clear image of the future they desire; otherwise, they have nowhere to lead their people.

Visionless Churches

The result of a visionless leader is a local church characterized by spiritual malaise, lethargy, and nostalgia for the "good ol' days." A church that lacks a clearly communicated and compelling vision will lack a healthy sense of identity as a church. When the vision of a church is clear, people will be able to cite the vision as the primary reason they do (or do not) attend that church. Former-pastor-turned-vision-coach Will Mancini makes the case that without a clear vision, church members will attach themselves to the building, to the pastor, to their favorite programs, or to a small, close-knit group of people in the church—and will be less open and even resistant to change.

A visionless church can exist for a very long time, seemingly unaffected. But if you watch and listen carefully, its activities, concerns, and conversations will be increasingly about itself. Thom Rainer calls this preoccupation with self "inward drift." He says that churches can exist "for years and even decades with inward drift. The church may not be making disciples… but its members and constituents are willing to fund the congregation since it meets their perceived needs and desires."[2]

Robert Dale wrote about churches that lacked vision in *To Dream Again*. Dale explained that a compelling vision leads to meaningful ministry and growth. But as the church ages, the vision will naturally begin to fade, causing the church to plateau in size and effectiveness. If vision is not renewed, that church will begin the downward slope of decline, eventually leading to dropout or even organizational death. The key is to cast new vision at the top of the arc, *before* the downward fade begins.[3]

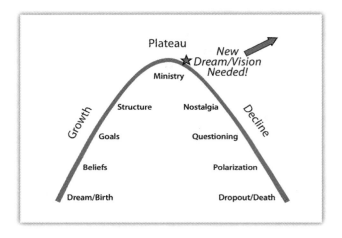

Finding Vision

If a church lacks vision, where can they find it? Vision comes from God. It would be a scary thing indeed if God left us to come up with our own plans and schemes for reaching the world. The relevant next question, then, is how does God go about *revealing* his vision to a local church?

God established the church as a community of faith, so it's no surprise that vision is revealed and implemented in a similar way—through a Spirit-led group process. (Note the frequency of plural words used to describe the early church's leadership: Acts 6:3-4; 11:30; 14:23; 20:17, 28; Philippians 1:1; 1 Timothy 5:17; Titus 1:5; Hebrews 13:17; James 5:14; 1 Peter 5:1.) A pastor should have an influential role but within a system of

plural leadership—whether accountable to a group
of leaders or in a "first among equals" arrangement.
This reflects the wisdom of Proverbs 15:22: "Plans go
wrong for lack of counsel; many advisers bring success."
However these relational influences function in a local
church, we should most often expect that God will
reveal ministry plans through the community of faith.

When leaders gather to discern God's vision for their
church, they should look carefully at the intersection of
three elements: 1) God's will; 2) community needs and
desires; 3) the uniqueness of the local church.[4]

1. **God's will:** God has revealed himself and his will
   in the Bible. We cannot summarize that good and
   perfect will here, but among many other things,
   God desires that people love and worship him;
   that people be invited to follow Jesus and be
   discipled in Jesus' way; that the oppressed receive
   mercy; that the hungry be fed and the widow and
   the orphan be cared for.

2. **Local needs and desires:** To be useful, the vision
   must be anchored within a local community. A
   church that says "Our vision is to see people
   believe in Jesus" has only demonstrated contextual
   ignorance; it is the mission of every church to see
   people become Christians. The proper question
   is "How does God want to use our church to
   lead people into a commitment to Jesus *in this
   community?*" Examine the community around the

church. Who are your neighbors? What are their needs, fears, concerns, pains, and burdens? Look closely, ask questions, and, most of all, *listen*.

3. **Uniqueness of the local church:** Examine your church. Who are you? What are the backgrounds of the people in your faith family? What are the predominant gifts, passions, and abilities of your people? This is why it is always a bad idea for one church to simply imitate another, more successful, church. The body of Christ is made up of many parts, each of them unique. Find and deploy the unique people who are parts of your church.

God's Will

Local Needs & Desires

VISION!

Uniqueness of the Local Church

At the intersection of these three categories is the sweet spot of God's vision for your local church! Pastors, staff, lay leaders, and congregation members need to work together to find it. This will not be easy or quick, but as you earnestly pray together, get to know your community, and make an honest assessment of yourselves, God will reveal his vision for your church!

By Brian Walton

VISION: THE FOUNDATION OF CHANGE

COMMUNICATING VISION

After developing the vision for your church, your task as leader is to effectively communicate that preferred future. Keep in mind that "change is not made without inconvenience, even from worse to better."[5] Some people in your congregation will be ready for the new vision and all it entails. Some will come on board with a little coaxing. Others will need more convincing. Still others may resist at every juncture. Your job will be to stay "on message" with all of them, while working to build trust and commitment for the new direction.

"Effective communicator" and "inspiring motivator" are two key roles of effective leaders. Add to that the fundamental leadership qualities of "passionate about the mission" and "interpersonal sensitivity,"[6] and you have an excellent framework for what to do in communicating your vision—you must be articulate, motivational, passionate, and relational. Your job is to present ideas in such a way that you engage hearts and minds. People want to be part of something that matters, something that makes a difference. People are desperate for meaning and a sense of purpose in their lives—so inspire them!

Pastoral Communication

As you and your team roll out your vision, one of your challenges will be to continually communicate three ideas, two of which are: 1) God is constant; and 2) the purpose of the church (to call people to know, love, and follow Jesus) stays the same. The third idea is where the challenge comes in; namely, our methods (the implementation of vision) must change. Help your people see the positive aspects of embracing new ideas, while finding comfort in a God who is ultimately in control.

For Christians, this communication must also be shaped by scriptural principles. Kindness, compassion, humility, and patience should be marks of how we interact with others (Colossians 3:12), even with those who might disagree with us. As leaders, we are also told to be prepared "whether the time is favorable or not. Patiently correct, rebuke, and encourage your people with good teaching" (2 Timothy 4:2). While not being "quarrelsome," we are still to balance accountability with encouragement, support with tenacity (1 Thessalonians 5:14; 2 Timothy 2:24).

Communication does not simply mean preaching at people. It involves speaking and listening, formal teaching moments and one-on-one chats, written materials (such as articles, newsletters, blogs, emails), and social media discussions. Know your audience and how they best give and receive information. What emotional language do they speak? Be intentional about your wording.

There are many conversations happening in your church: from you to your congregation; from your congregation back to you and your leadership team; from one member to another; from members to their friends. Ensuring that all this back-and-forth messaging is consistent requires focus, repetition, and simplicity.

What you ultimately want is for people to be convinced, over time, that the shared vision for the future can become reality with God's help. You are aiming for ownership, not just buy-in. As Bill Hybels says, "When people own a vision—people will pray for it, root for it, advocate for it, give to it, volunteer in it, protect it, will sacrifice for it, die for it."[7]

> Help your people see the positive aspects of embracing new ideas, while finding comfort in a God who is ultimately in control.

Repetition, Repetition, Repetition

People are distracted. According to marketing research, it takes five to nine times of hearing a message for someone to act on it—*if* they are paying attention. For a distracted audience, it would take many more repetitions before you get a response. You can reduce that number by speaking clearly and with conviction!

In *Managing Transitions: Making the Most of Change*, author William Bridges says that in order to help people let go of the old in order to embrace the new, you must give people information and do it again and again, while telling them what is ending and what is not. He goes on to say that as you launch the new vision, you not only spend time clarifying and communicating the purpose but you help paint a picture of the future that people can relate to and engage with.[8]

The proven formula for getting people's attention and inspiring them is to find creative ways to tell people what's at stake so they care. In an article in the *Harvard Business Review,* authors Jim Collins and Jerry Porras call this "vivid description—that is, a vibrant, engaging, and specific description of what it will be like to achieve" your goals, using "passion, emotion, and conviction."[9] Create a set of rich, colorful pictures that people cannot easily forget.

Improving your communication and presentation skills is vital. Do you make good eye contact? Use pleasant facial expressions? Make good use of hand gestures and tone of voice? Author Craig Chappelow cites a study published in Claremont McKenna College's *Leadership Review* that says that these abilities (which can be learned and practiced) matter, as does specific wording: "Inclusive language such as 'we,' 'us,' and 'our,' (instead of 'they') tended to unify people to the vision."[10]

Jesus was a great vision communicator. He was clear on his purpose for being here. He was direct in much of his communication and was not swayed by others' criticisms. He also was a master of word pictures to get his point across. The subject of the kingdom of God alone shows Jesus using stories about seeds, yeast, a sower, a great banquet, and the ten talents.

> Use every opportunity, day in and day out, to talk about the vision—not just at large meetings and special gatherings. Find ways to link everything to the vision and get people animated and talking about it.

John Kotter, a Harvard Business School professor, developed an eight-step change model that indicates reiteration is important, as is enthusiasm. Use every opportunity, day in and day out, to talk about the vision—not just at large meetings and special gatherings.[11] Find ways to link everything to the vision and get people animated and talking about it. The most successful leaders also "make it a point to frequently engage in private, one-on-one or small group dialogues with their constituents at every level."[12] Although face-to-face conversations can be time-consuming, they clarify and build deeper commitment, ensuring that true meaning is received and embraced. Seek out various stakeholders: those who stand to benefit; those who may lose the most; those who can help lead the change; those who can implement the change; and opinion leaders in your congregation. Take time to address concerns but don't focus exclusively on the loudest naysayers. Be "inspirational and practicable... Often this will require *over-communication* through multiple, redundant channels."[13]

Communication Strategy

Here are some things to consider as you develop a communication plan.

- Brainstorm with your team key words and phrases; agree on using consistent descriptions.

- Practice telling the important points in five minutes or less; focus on the one or two things you want people to remember.

- Design and practice your presentation(s) with specific audiences in mind.

- Seek out and schedule two-way conversation opportunities with various stakeholders.

- Create attractive visual aids (sermon slides, PowerPoint presentations, brochures, website banners, and bulletin announcements).

- Generate a list of frequently asked questions—and come up with answers in advance.

- Be honest, enthusiastic, and passionate.
- Don't condemn the past.
- Don't lose sight of your vision and why things need to change.
- Stay connected to God and to your support network.

Remember that words are powerful. As you carefully select the words you use to convey a compelling vision, keep in mind that God is ultimately the one who, through the work of his Holy Spirit, brings about lasting change.

"And my message and my preaching were very plain. Rather than using clever and persuasive speeches, I relied only on the power of the Holy Spirit. I did this so you would trust not in human wisdom but in the power of God."

— 1 Corinthians 2:4-5

By Shirley Giles Davis

IMPLEMENTING VISION

You have an inspiring vision. You are clear on what and how and to whom you need to communicate. Now it's time to lead, to translate your vision into reality. In implementing a new vision, you are asking people to think or behave differently. For many, this may require overcoming fears; for all, it will require a time of learning and adjustment.

As a first step, think strategically about creating a team to help implement and sustain the vision. This could be your staff and elders. This could be an ad hoc group of opinion leaders in your congregation. The goal is to have people who are respected by many and have different spheres of influence. Choose people who work well together and are committed to see the process all the way through. Be sure they all share the same clear expectations.

Planning Your First Steps

Once you have a team and have developed your communication strategy, your next step is to create a detailed plan. Ask:

- Where are we now, where do we want to be, and how do we get there?

- How will we involve everyone in the conversation and the effort? Can we identify influencers who can help with messaging?

- What can we do to encourage ownership?

- How ready is our organization for this change? What are the major barriers—are they practical, cultural, emotional, political, financial, behavioral? How do we remove those barriers? How do we increase people's readiness?

- Who will gain the most from the proposed change? Who will feel the greatest sense of loss?

- How will we track our plans and assign responsibility?

John Kotter's eight-step change model is a useful planning tool. Step 1 is to create urgency—create the kind of buzz that gets people looking forward

> See the "How to Change" chapter in this book for more details on the change process.

to the envisioned future. Kotter says that 75 percent of an organization's leadership needs to "buy into the change"[14] in order for it to be successful, so spend the time and energy to win leaders over first.

Getting everyone on board and moving in the same direction is fundamental to any implementation plan. According to Jim Collins and Jerry Porras, authors of *Built to Last*, "building a visionary company requires 1% vision and 99% alignment."[15] Unfortunately, people tend to be comfortable with the status quo. Therefore, in order for a ministry vision to take root, it needs to permeate all levels of the church. It's important for the leaders to align the vision and plan with the church's values and to applaud places of congruence.

Nehemiah's Vision for Jerusalem

The Old Testament leader Nehemiah provides an excellent case study for vision implementation. In the book of Nehemiah, we see him personally consumed with the problem of Jerusalem in ruins and seeking God in fervent prayer (Nehemiah 1:4-11). Our visions for our churches should begin in much the same way, with a nudge from the Holy Spirit that creates passion which, in turn, drives us to seek God's guidance before moving ahead.

Next, Nehemiah developed a preliminary plan. Before beginning any work, Nehemiah fully assessed what was needed. When his inspection was complete, Nehemiah inspired first the leaders and then the people that the city wall could and must be rebuilt—by them. As a result of his passionate appeal, work began (Nehemiah 2:7-18). William Bridges, author of *Managing Transitions*, says that keys to helping people in this uncertain phase include having a plan and giving people roles to play in the process.

> Our visions for our churches should begin… with a nudge from the Holy Spirit that creates passion which, in turn, drives us to seek God's guidance.

Unfortunately, as with many visions, Nehemiah's team encountered real threats. But because Nehemiah had been involved and informed, he kept the plan on course and reassured the people by responding quickly to contingencies, such as protecting the workers from enemy attack. He was visible and available when they needed him to be. He changed the workload and the teams to accommodate any surprises (Nehemiah 2:19-20; 3–4). To achieve enduring change, leaders must continually cast and recast vision, *especially* during times of confusion and turmoil.

Preparing for Pushback

When creating your implementation plan, don't overlook readiness and resistance. Doing a readiness assessment is an important step. How ready are your people for this new future? If their level(s) of discontent with the status quo are not high or if you have not yet clearly painted a tangible picture of where you are headed, your congregation may not feel ready to make the change. Author Seth Godin writes:

> There's a myth that all you need to do is outline your vision and prove it's

right—then, quite suddenly, people will line up and support you. In fact, the opposite is true. Remarkable visions and genuine insight are always met with resistance.[16]

Nehemiah faced internal opposition in the form of quarreling factions. He provided strong leadership while mediating these delicate situations by calling people to be their best, gaining their cooperation, and earning their respect (Nehemiah 5). How will you address opposition? One way to detour opposition is to identify and highlight small "wins" early in the change process. This will engage people who are less enthusiastic and advance the vision where it's most receptive.

See the "Anticipating Responses to Change" chapter in this book for more details on resistance to change.

Nehemiah did not allow ever-increasing conflict to distract him from his purpose. He was a consistent vision caster with a plan that took into account all contingencies. He had a solid confidence in God. The result: "People worked with all their heart" in spite of outside pressures. The outcome of Nehemiah's leadership, vision, faith, and clear strategy is seen in Nehemiah 6:15: "So…the wall was finished—just fifty-two days after we had begun."

IMPLEMENTING VISION

Integrating Your Vision

As you make progress on implementing the vision, continue talking about it constantly. Make vision language part of your everyday conversations, your preaching points, newsletters, worship bulletins, and social media. When you hire new staff, be sure it is part of the interview and training process. When new ministry leaders are chosen, orient them immediately to the vision. Of course, the best way to build and sustain commitment is for you and your leadership team to model it yourselves.

Your biggest role as leader is to stick with the vision for the long run and to help your congregation do the same until it becomes instinctive to all. You will know you have accomplished this when the people most affected by the changes act, think, and behave in ways consistent with the vision.

> Stick with the vision for the long run and... help your congregation do the same until it becomes instinctive.

In the end, keep God at the center—personally and corporately. Remind yourself and your people that God will ultimately accomplish *his* purposes: "Lord, you will grant us peace; all we have accomplished is really from you" (Isaiah 26:12). Be a vision implementer after the pattern of Nehemiah: passionate, prayerful, faithful. Be one who has a plan—but is open to amending that plan. Know your culture and context. Love your people well, and call them to a great unified task. Remove the hindrances. Inspire them. Keep casting vision and communicating. Show integrity. May you look back and be able to say, "Vision accomplished!"

By Shirley Giles Davis

IMPLEMENTING VISION

WHO CAN LEAD CHANGE

"Sometimes I wish I could receive the same clean slate I constantly give others," Rob confessed to his wife, Nancy.

"What do you mean?" Nancy asked. "Is this about what we talked about yesterday regarding people who have left?" This was their third late-night conversation in as many days about church.

"Sort of, but it's not so much about them rejecting me as their pastor as it is about me feeling like I can't do anything significant anymore."

Nancy nodded empathetically, "I can tell this is really bothering you. What do you think is going on?"

Rob paused, "It's ironic, actually. When we came here eight years ago, I had all the slack in the world to lead change. The problem was I didn't know what needed to be done or how to do it back then. But now that I've learned about this church and actually know the people, it doesn't seem to matter. I feel less able to lead real change now than I did back then."

"Is it really that bad? You don't have any ideas?"

"All I know is I feel that others would rather correct my style than consider my ideas," he said. "I'll say something, and then I'll hear how I should've presented it a different way...or not presented it at all and let someone else bring it up...or been more hands-off... or been more hands-on. They focus on the 10 percent they think I'm shortsighted on versus the 90 percent I'm probably spot-on about."

Nancy listened, remaining silent.

Rob stood up and walked over to a nearby window, looking outside, "I wonder sometimes if I should quit. I can't seem to change anything or anyone here. Maybe I'd be better off in some other church where people have never seen my learning curve and wouldn't be distracted by it. Nancy, I really have some good ideas to share that can help change the church. They're not perfect, but they're a solid start. What's the point of even trying, though?"

The Qualities of a Change Agent

All leaders struggle on some level with having valuable insights and ideas that others aren't yet willing to appreciate. For every leap of faith you might ask people to take on an intangible vision, they have rock-solid memories and potent emotions associated with when you were previously shortsighted. You could attempt to counter this by pointing out the victories you *have* had, hoping your good moments can outweigh the bad. Unfortunately, this tends to merely create a louder argument with no real long-term solution.

The secret to leading real change is found in Scripture: "The human body has many parts, but the many parts make up one whole body. So it is with the body of Christ...All of you together are Christ's body, and each of you is a part of it" (1 Corinthians 12:12, 27).

According to this passage, the union of the various parts of the body doesn't just form the idea or institution of the church; rather, Christ himself is somehow more fully revealed. This distinction means everything, for only Jesus can permanently transform a person, group of people, or situation. Any lasting change must be rooted in him.

Wherever Christ-centered transformation occurs, then, we should expect to find a variety of change agents at work. At the church leadership level, this truth is confirmed by the fact that people respond best to their favorite type of leader. Each leader has individual strengths that stand out but which must collectively work with other strengths to bring about meaningful change. Some of these different types of change agents might include:

- *Future-talker:* A leader who can identify and reveal the way things "could be" and "should be."

- *Strategy maker:* Someone who can create the right steps that will take everyone from A to Z.

WHO CAN LEAD CHANGE

- *Process manager:* An implementer who knows how to organize people and resources into the strategy.

- *Team mobilizer:* A talent scout who puts the right people into the right roles so that the right thing can happen at the right time.

- *People-lover:* An encourager known for building community.

- *Finger-pointer:* A prophetic voice who can practically help stuck or misguided people know what the right next step is.

- *Character reminder:* A holistic individual who helps everyone remember who they're supposed to be while doing what needs to be done.

- *Urgency-producer:* A pacesetter who lets everyone know what needs to be done right now.

- *First-follower:* An inspirational person who leads by a faithful, bold example of support.

These skills and knowledge are obviously not limited to pastors alone but can be contributed by lay church members. Some leaders might be able to fulfill several roles, but it's doubtful any one person can take on all of them. (Pastors, take heed.) Each type can foster some measure of change, even those that aren't typically considered to be leadership qualities. This is where the change process will stall if the leadership role is not defined broadly or shared among several people.

For example, you may have once been thought of in your church as a certain type of leader but now no longer seem to effectively serve in that capacity. That doesn't necessarily mean it's time to move on from your church. Perhaps you could now be in a different change agent role. What if, instead of insisting upon doing some tasks you performed in the past, you used this time to empower someone else to serve, for the sake of the future? Even if your church lacks people to fill all the necessary roles, you can supplement your resources through books, consultants, or conferences.

> Only Jesus can permanently transform a person, group of people, or situation. Any lasting change must be rooted in him.

Officially (and Unofficially) Speaking

Change is fostered formally and informally. In a formal-oriented system or structure, change travels via top-down positional authority. In an informal setting, change percolates through grassroots-level relationships, eventually affecting the whole organization. The structure itself can be misleading, though, as change frequently occurs in formal and informal ways in all types of organizations. For example, some church officials may never carry as much influence as does a particular congregation member whom everyone respects. Likewise, a group of lay people attempting to enact change may not gain traction until an official authority figure adds his or her endorsement.

It's clear that change can originate with or be cultivated by many people in a variety of positions. So remember to value anyone who can contribute toward change, including often overlooked groups of people such as:

- *Spouses:* Leadership teams (staff, boards, committees) should gather at least quarterly with spouses included. Whether it's a fun activity together or brainstorming important matters, honoring spouses and their input can create greater camaraderie at home and church-wide.

- *Students:* Regularly invite sharp students into important meetings that involve the future of the church. You might include students as young as 8th or 9th grade. And don't forget college students who call your church their home (even though you might not see them regularly on Sunday mornings). Consider their input with as much weight as you would give any congregation member.

- *Seniors:* Allow the retired to get "refired" by having them share about the values that have shaped their spiritual journeys. Give them space in weekend services to share relevant stories of transformation that will inspire others.

- *Non–church-members:* Before you plan your next outdoor activity or building campaign, take into consideration the people who live around your church. Solicit their input on what would serve the neighborhood, along with any ways your church can connect with their households.

Value anyone who can contribute toward change, including often overlooked groups of people.

Congregational change can be fully realized only when Christians come together as the body of Christ. A pastor's task in this endeavor is not to embody every leadership characteristic but to "equip God's people to do his work and build up the church, the body of Christ" (Ephesians 4:12). The more people you can include in the process of seeking God together, the more likely you will realize not just a human-sized vision but a God-sized revelation that results in positive, lasting change.

By Tony Myles

WHO CAN LEAD CHANGE

WHAT TO CHANGE

Does your church show signs of needing change? Not just tweaking the coffee flavors or carpet color but the intentional kind that takes time, thought, effort, and teamwork to implement. Consider these questions to focus change on the areas that need it.

- **Is your church growing?** You might need to change the current structure by adding to staff, volunteers, or your building before the growth is stifled.

- **Is your church *not* growing?** If you're maintaining the status quo or declining, you might need to investigate who is leaving and why. Or find out what community factors might be hindering growth. The findings might require changes in ministry philosophy or reallocation of resources.

- **Are people bringing ideas to you, excited about future possibilities?** As you hear common themes, the direction of your change might become clear.

- **Are most celebrations, stories, and benchmarks referred to in the past tense?** If "we used to," "that was never a problem before," and "we've always…" become the prevailing phrases, the change you need is a new initiative that will create new memories and stories.

- **Are there unhealthy relationships among your staff, volunteers, and members?** Unhealthy relationships among staff members are a warning sign that you need to reorganize your staff. Friction between congregational members might indicate the church's purpose and direction aren't clear, which causes people to meander in various directions and end up in conflict with each other.

Determining Targets for Change

Not everything can be changed at once. Nor *should* everything be changed at once. Narrow your focus even further than the list above by considering the possibilities and creating a list of essentials and priorities. A good first step is to gather input from your congregation. Use this table to begin the process.

	Possibilities	Benefits	Importance (1-10)
Facilities			
Staff			
Ministry Structure			
Leadership Structure			
Communication			

Technology			
Involvement			
Community Impact			
Spiritual Growth			
Other			
Other			

Ask several trusted people who understand the mission and culture of the congregation to test the evaluation. Based on their feedback and the results of their evaluations, revise the table as needed. For example, you might want to get more information about your ministry structure, assessing the specifics of oversight, responsibilities, and expectations. Avoid getting too specific, though, because you want people to keep the big picture in mind as they are assessing. Keep the perspective broad throughout the evaluation process; then let the results reveal the priorities. Also, take care not to let your personal agenda drive the assessment tool.

For maximum return rates, distribute the evaluations at an all-church meeting, either a regular service time or at a meeting designated for this purpose. Have everyone

WHAT TO CHANGE

complete and return the evaluations then and there. If that is impractical, send evaluations home with your people, giving them a specific time frame to complete the evaluation.

Shorter time frames usually work best; otherwise, some people will set it aside, thinking they have plenty of time to complete it, but then forget it among more pressing tasks. As the deadline approaches, send a quick reminder to everyone, such as: "Thanks to everyone who has completed the evaluation that will help us see where we are as we set priorities for moving forward. If you haven't submitted yours, please get it to me by the end of the day tomorrow. I value your input and don't want to miss it." Relationships are important. Establish and maintain healthy lines of communication.

Calculate all the results. (Remember to complete one for yourself, too.) See what priorities rise to the top, based on the possibilities and benefits. Be sure to give feedback. While you might not be able to give specifics to everyone, you can provide general information, such as: "We've put your responses together, and you've helped identify several things that need to change. Please continue to pray as we consider the next steps and best timing for change in each area."

Outside perspectives and suggestions can be valuable in deciding what changes your church should make.

Outsiders' Opinions

Besides congregational input, outside perspectives and suggestions can be valuable in deciding what changes your church should make. General church research is easily found in all sorts of religious publications and websites that can point out needs and preferences that your church should be aware of, as well as ministry models you might want to adopt. Denominational offices and overseers can also give you some feedback that might be more objective than your own opinion. Even neighbors who live near your church property can provide insights into what might need to change in your church.

It's easy to discount suggestions for change made by people outside your church; after all, they aren't as familiar with your particular situation as you are. However, just because you find a few minor details that don't apply, don't discount such change suggestions altogether.

"The mind of a person with understanding gets knowledge; the wise person listens to learn more."

—Proverbs 18:15, New Century Version

WHAT TO CHANGE

The Ripple Effect

Once you're able to focus on two or three main areas of change, you can consider the requirements of change, as well as the impact of it. When you change something in one area of the church, it will probably have a ripple effect, so some of the areas you might rank with a low priority might end up with some change after all.

For example, technology might be assessed as a low priority, while communications is near the top. Some communications don't require technology. (Believe it or not, we can actually walk up to someone and talk face to face.) However, in order to communicate in efficient and effective ways, technology is essential. You may not need the best system and software money can buy, but the rationalization of "it was good enough ten years ago, so it's good enough now" doesn't work when it comes to technology. People who didn't have a cellphone ten years ago now do. The person who said they'd never text now prefers to communicate primarily by text. The person who adamantly spoke of the evils of social media now admits to using it ("but just because I don't want to miss out on what's going on in my family"). If you want to improve your communication (high priority), you need to consider how people communicate and then adjust your technology (lower priority) accordingly.

Handling the Conflict of Change

Determining areas of change often creates conflict. It is essential that you have a clear vision or purpose before beginning the change process. When you do, you can filter every decision through that vision or purpose. Church-wide decisions aren't personal; they are purposeful. However, realize that the decisions will *feel* personal to many. Be cautious about letting programs eclipse people. You might find yourself making decisions about programs in order to accomplish the vision, but remember that good vision has people intricately woven through it. God cares about people—bringing them together, helping them know him, and challenging them to grow, worship, and serve.

As you decide what to change, be aware of the programs, rooms, decorations, benefits, or time frames that some might hold sacred. Try to anticipate the effects of changes that can create a firestorm of issues when they are enacted. Avoiding conflict is not a reason to maintain status quo, but disrupting the status quo just for the sake of change itself isn't a good reason to eliminate or change it either.

Filter the proposed change through the vision, and consider the people involved. Use wisdom, compassion, and sacrifice as you determine what to change. You don't have to find every piece of the puzzle and know where and when to click each one into place before

WHAT TO CHANGE

you start. Trust God to guide you as you take one step at a time into the shaky but exciting journey of change.

By Susan Lawrence

WHEN TO CHANGE

"I guess I'll sum it up if no one else will," Cory stated. "It feels like we're stuck." No one in the room seemed to disagree with his conclusion.

Jeff was the exception. "I don't think it's quite that dramatic," he said. "The circumstances are just different now. We got into this building by necessity when the movie theater we used to meet in closed. It was the best deal at the time, and we've certainly made the most of it."

"That may be," Cory countered, "but we've poured money into this facility to make it functional. That adds up to thousands of dollars that we'll never get back on something we don't even own. I don't think we should renew our lease, but we don't have the savings to go out and buy property for something new. We're stuck."

Pastor Chris wasn't sure if he should speak, having been at the church only six months. After an awkward pause, he commented, "As I understand the history of this, the last change was made out of necessity. We're now talking about making a change out of choice. That alone means we have some time to process this."

"No offense, pastor," Cory replied, "but we've all been having this conversation long before you came and I'm tired of it. I have no interest in delaying this decision any further. If we can't determine something as simple as meeting space, how are we ever going to determine the more important spiritual things?"

"What if this *is* a spiritual decision?" Jeff offered. "The Bible frequently mentions tabernacles and temples and worship being important to God. Why should this be any different? Shouldn't we take our time on this, however long it takes?"

Cory sighed, "I don't know how this sounds…but honestly, I have no interest in being a part of this church much longer if we're going to keep dragging our feet on the same things all the time."

Four Questions Before You Consider Change

Identifying the right time to change something always seems clearer from the outside looking in than from the inside. When you're in the thick of something, there are patterns of thinking and blind spots you won't be aware of. And the areas you *are* aware of can be equally debilitating because there always seems to be one more thing to consider, which, if overlooked, could bring everything tumbling down. At least, this is what you fear.

You need a tool or method to help decide if the time is right to move from the known present to the uncertain future. When you have both the freedom and capacity to consider change, here are four key questions to ask, summed up in the acronym B.R.A.P.[17]

Biblical. Does the proposed change reflect values that flow from Scripture?

Not everything you'll ever consider is explicitly spelled out in the Bible (such as a new educational wing or upgrades to the sound system), but the values supporting your idea need to be biblical. Take care that you don't try to validate a clever idea by stretching a Bible verse beyond its limits. Make sure there is an unforced, clear link between Scripture and whatever is being proposed.

Relational. Does the idea nurture community?

Churches may say they value relationships, but their actions will reveal if they truly love people and use things or use people and love things. Any proposed change in your church should not hinder dialogue and interpersonal connections. In fact, positive change should improve and strengthen your congregational relationships.

Accessible. Will the change process and the final result involve anyone who wants to participate?

Big changes tend to develop language and values that only the core leaders understand. This may be necessary in certain situations, but generally you're going to want as much ownership among as many different people as possible. Even if they won't have a hands-on role, make sure your congregation is informed about the big picture and that they understand the anticipated outcomes.

Professional. Does the proposed change foster credibility and respect by the way it will be handled?

Some people give their absolute best because they serve in a church. (It's for God's glory, right?) However, others may be sloppy or lazy because they serve in a church. (God's grace isn't based on our performance, right?) Pay attention to the details, and cast a vision for excellence that challenges the attitude of "good enough" among staff and lay volunteers.

When these four questions have been answered satisfactorily, you will know that the church is ready to begin making lasting changes. Your diligent attention to timing can enable the vision to be realized.

Preparing Your Church

Arguably, no church is ever completely ready for change. Facing the need for change can be tiring—physically, emotionally, and spiritually. Pastors can succumb to this just as easily as anyone. What might help is a method for people to process the proposed change through a season of conversation and inquiry. Wait to enact change until each group has understood, discussed, and accepted the plan. This could take weeks or months, depending on the group and degree of change being considered. For example:

- Pastoral/church leadership
- Staff and support leadership
- Families of leadership
- Church membership
- Community

When the pastoral and/or church leadership has accepted and committed to the change, then it is time for the staff and support leadership to get on board. Once they are committed, the plan can go to the families of leadership and on to each group in turn. You may have different groups or may want to overlap the discussion times.

Deciding when to start this process is also important. People generally respond well to large change in January (the beginning of the year), June (the end of the school year), and September (the beginning of the school year). Churches that observe the seasons of the Christian calendar might also find Advent, Lent, Eastertide, or Pentecost to be good times to enter into the change process. You'll also want to take note of other factors in the lifespan of a church that will help you identify its readiness for change:

WHEN TO CHANGE

- Have we taught people how to pray and seek God beyond personal desires?

- Are there any side issues at play that are unrelated to what's being proposed but will likely distract the conversations?

- Is everyone on board with a biblical method of how we will handle disagreements?

- When was the last "big ask" or change proposed to the church, such as a building campaign or ministry restructuring? Is the congregation worn out from it all or ready for something new?

Timing makes a deep impact on ministry. You can't afford to wait for perfect circumstances that may never arrive; nor can you overlook opportunities that can strengthen your church when they arise. God can use anything to accomplish his purposes, but we do have a say in our preparation, which can make God's job easy or difficult.

> You can't afford to wait for perfect circumstances that may never arrive; nor can you overlook opportunities that can strengthen your church when they arise.

Clarifying the Real Issue

Inherent in the human side of all this is the question "What's in it for me?" Members of your church may not be willing to move forward until they feel that question has been answered to their satisfaction. You can respond by providing them with good data that helps them see how their contribution will matter in the grand scheme of things.

Even better would be to point to the ultimate goal by helping people ask and answer "What's in this for God?" This question may change even the way you make decisions, from casting votes in a majority-wins system to praying until everyone reaches consensus. It may take longer to seek the will of God than listening to the loudest human voices, but it will create a better foundation for lasting change that matters.

By Tony Myles

WHAT NOT TO CHANGE

What pastor wouldn't love free rein to make whatever changes he or she wanted? No financial limits, no board of elders approval needed, no negative reactions from the congregation. Where would you start, and what might be the possibilities?

Unfortunately, real-life change is inhibited by economics, building and space issues, and relationships with staff, governing authorities, and church members. Yet, all churches will undergo change eventually. Some changes are necessary and unavoidable, while others are beneficial but optional. A third category includes those changes that *should not* be made—or made rarely and only after considerable reflection. Knowing what changes fall into this third category is vital for the wise pastor.

The Anatomy of Change: Spine Issues

The non-negotiable things that shouldn't be changed may involve matters of doctrine or worship or programs and ministries. Some may be so vital, they *can't* be changed. These are all "spine" issues. We need our spines to stand upright—and to do just about anything. They not only give us structure and support but they hold the critical communication system of nerves that run throughout our bodies. If the spine is broken, we're immobilized.

The spine issues are the biblical truths that do not change: God is eternally existent in three persons, Father, Son, and Holy Spirit; Jesus is the Son of God, who lived on earth, died, and overcame death so that people can receive forgiveness of sins and eternal life through him; the Bible is the inspired, authoritative Word of God. These and other biblical truths provide critical structure and support to the lives of individuals and churches. No local church or pastor has the authority to change these vital vertebrae.

If your church belongs to a denomination, other doctrinal distinctives may be considered spine issues. Flowing from these theological convictions may be certain forms of church government, financial structures and procedures, and even some programs that are required by your denomination. There may be avenues for making change through representative-based groups such as synods, conferences, or districts. These channels move slowly, but any resulting change can be far-reaching and significant. However, local churches have no authority or power to change these spine issues on their own, so no decision is necessary.

"Hold on to the pattern of wholesome teaching you learned from me—a pattern shaped by the faith and love that you have in Christ Jesus. Through the power of the Holy Spirit who lives within us, carefully guard the precious truth that has been entrusted to you."

—2 Timothy 1:13-14

The Anatomy of Change: Expendable Ribs

Closely related—connected even—are the ribs. Ribs protect vital organs and give us structure so that we're not a floppy mess of skin. An important distinction from the spine is that we can live without a rib or two. If a rib is broken, we can usually still function. It might be painful and inconvenient but not life-threatening. Furthermore, some ribs are more expendable than others. We need to know the difference between spine and rib issues.

In ministry terms, rib issues are connected to the spine, but they're not as essential. Rib issues can be the source of heated debate which can, in turn, easily lead to divisions. While we don't want to throw out all the rib issues, we also don't want to stubbornly claim they can't be changed. Some structures and rules don't need to be permanent or universal if they are rib-related.

For example, we might believe baptism can only happen in one particular mode in one special place and only at certain times. While our practice might have biblical support, other passages or interpretations support other ways of baptizing.

We might feel the same way about programs and ministries, such as Sunday school classes: "We've always done them this way, and if we don't continue, people won't know God's Word." When we make such sweeping statements, we need to be open to the possibility that we're dealing with a rib issue. The alternatives we face usually aren't as drastic as keeping Sunday school exactly the way it is, on one hand, or getting rid of it altogether, on the other hand. In between, there are many options for change, as long as they all help people learn God's Word.

At times, rib issues can seem just as critical as spine issues. In fact, some issues are difficult to tell apart. Many local churches have established mission statements and lists of core values. Can these be changed without drastically affecting the nature and identity of that church? Your answer to that question might be a clue to whether you're dealing with spine or rib issues.

Some structures and rules don't need to be permanent or universal.

Guide to Rib Surgery

Assuming you have correctly identified some "ribs" that should be changed or removed, you also need to know if the conditions are right for the operation. If they aren't just right, the patient might not survive the procedure, so you shouldn't make the change. This often means asking about the qualifications of those leading the change (the surgical team) and whether the costs are bearable.

Check your own motives. Why do you want to change something? Do you want to do things your way or prove yours is the right way? Why do you want to avoid changing something? Do you want to avoid conflict or boredom? If your motives are self-serving, change won't be beneficial, even if it's a positive change. Acknowledge your personal agenda and shred it—literally. Write down everything you want to happen (or not happen) as you face change. Don't sugarcoat it. Be honest. Then commit it to God, and put your preferences through the shredder. If these motives creep back into your thinking in the following days and weeks, perhaps you should rethink the need for change.

Be aware of other people. Change isn't just about content; it's a process that involves and affects people. Especially be aware of key people who influence others. Unhealthy change-leaders can contaminate the process, making the results unhealthy, too. Of course, you cannot fix every relational and leadership issue in the church before implementing change; otherwise, change would never happen. Nor can you control other people's motives and responses. But you can be aware of them.

Some people are energized by conflict, and your introduction of change might be just the fuel they need to get up in arms. Other people thrive on attention. With the availability of social media, it's not difficult to get it. Some people are passive-aggressives. They might fly under your radar for a while, eventually exploding with damaging force. Take care that the key change-leaders are healthy in body, heart, mind, and spirit. If they are not, it's better not to start the change process.

> Unhealthy change-leaders can contaminate the process, making the results unhealthy, too.

Be cautious in what you change if you are new to the church. Get to know people. Ask questions. Figure out how communications and leadership work. There are usually two structures: the formal one, which you can see on an organization chart, and the informal one, which is just as influential and powerful. Observe closely to find the dynamics that impact the way people share and implement ideas.

Count the costs. Change is expensive. It's important to consider the financial impact of change, of course. You also need to consider the sacrifice of time and energy. Any minute spent discussing, planning, or even thinking about the change is a minute that can't be used for any other purpose. You will also need to make relational sacrifices. For example, change requires listening and sharing, which involves conversations with many people. Some conversations are energizing, but others can be draining. Avoid placing the costs and benefits in neat and tidy columns too quickly. You might see facing difficult conversations as an expensive cost, but it can also be a valuable investment as you build relationships. Many of these sacrifices are worth it, but it's important to consider the costs ahead of time. If the cost is too high, hold off on change.

By Susan Lawrence

HOW TO CHANGE

Dozens of books have been written on change strategies, and each approach seems to compete with the next. How can you know what to do? Try these important tips, regardless of the approach you take.

Tips for Making Changes

Communicate well. Good change cannot happen without good communication. Avoid seeing yourself as the keeper of all information. That's too much pressure for one person to control. Freely share your knowledge and plans (within the bounds of appropriateness and confidentiality). On the other hand, you don't need to tell everyone everything because that can be overwhelming. Different groups of people need differing amounts and kinds of information.

See the "Communicating Vision" chapter in this book for more details on communication in the change process.

Communicate with a variety of methods, because people learn in different ways. They need to hear, see, and engage in experiences that impact them personally. Personal experiences are more memorable and are more likely to lead to openness to new ideas than verbal or printed announcements alone.

Identify key people. People look to others for influence. You are not that person for everyone. Watch for those whom other people seem to follow. Especially consider different demographic groups. Who do the young married couples seem to gather around? To whom do the retirees look for support? Who usually seems busy with people around them asking for opinions and help? Whose names do you often hear as people share stories of who they trust? Take time to invest in these key people, answering their questions and sharing details about the change. The more they understand and own the process, the more they will help others understand and get excited about it.

Work with others.
Share ownership of the change process. If you are the only person who has decided on the change, you have missed out on valuable information. While you can't consider every person's perspective, it's important to invite some people into the process. The added questions, ideas, and strategies will facilitate the change process.

> See the "Who Can Lead Change" chapter in this book for more details on including other people in the change process.

Ask questions. Be critical…in a productive way. Ask questions of the change process, such as "What if…?"

and "How will that affect…?" Pursue questions and answers for as long as it is productive but be careful not to get bogged down with over-analyzing. Also, ask questions during the various stages of change, especially as people begin to process the change. Ask clarifying or follow-up questions, which can alert you to how important a concern is to someone or why someone seems to have a strong reaction against the change. When there is an emotional reaction to proposed changes, there is usually a deeper underlying reason. Take time to gently probe into these deeper issues.

Allow time. Some people thrive on change. It energizes them, and they can't wait to get started and see it through. Others take more time to warm up to new ideas. They need to ask questions, make a list of pros and cons, and even grieve over a lost or changed tradition. Neither approach is right or wrong, and both have strengths and weaknesses. You don't need to wait for every single person to jump on board, but do be considerate and patient with those who take more time. In the meantime, keep the eager beavers invested and excited by providing small ways to get involved early. For everyone's sake, continue to share the big picture and answer questions as they arise.

Skills for Leading Change

While certainly not exhaustive, this list provides an idea of essential skills for leading change. You might see

HOW TO CHANGE

some of your own personal weaknesses in one or more area. That doesn't disqualify you from leading change.

Once you are aware of a weakness, you can pay special attention to it. You can download an app to help you or put other reminders in place. You and your leadership team can complement each other. However, there are some skills that you cannot delegate. For instance, every leader needs to be a good listener. This comes more naturally to some than others, but everyone can develop better listening skills. Here's more:

- Stress management skills
- Mediation and conflict resolution skills
- Time management skills
- Goal-setting skills
- Reflection and evaluation skills
- Relational skills

Stages of Change

In an ideal life of a church, you will see a positive progression of development:

1. A few people see a vision and launch it.
2. Early adopters catch on to the purpose and help with the plan.
3. A variety of leaders step up to meet the goals.

4. Organizers and doers fill in the necessary gaps to make ministry work.

5. Servants continually step up to use their gifts and talents wherever and however needed.

You can probably see hints of each of these steps in your ministry. You likely see a few messes, confusions, and unfulfilled responsibilities, too.

Change isn't always progress. Some change is toward decline:

- People invest in the church and get comfortable. They get into a routine and like the stability.

- Those who question traditions, the status quo, and try to change things are viewed by others as hostile to the church.

- People begin to take sides, even if they weren't originally part of either group. The middle ground diminishes.

- People, including leaders, get frustrated. Their hope wanes. They get angry or indifferent.

- The church or ministry stagnates or dies.

Sadly, the negative progression happens more than it should. Although you can't control everything (and you're also not personally responsible for everything), these simple phrase-starters can help you guide change in a positive direction.

HOW TO CHANGE

- *If a church is going to change*…people must seek and follow God's will. There are no easy answers, no three-step process for successful change. It's going to look different for each church. It will even differ in the same church at different times. But humility and obedience are essential.

- *If a church is going to change*…thinking must change. People cannot continue to think the same way on the same things and expect to change, either in personal life or ministry. If leadership is not willing to change the way they think, those who follow won't be either. Just saying you want to change and putting new behaviors in place isn't enough. People will just go through the motions.

- *If a church is going to change*…attitudes must change. Thinking involves the mind, and attitudes involve the heart. Not only do people need to think differently, but they also need to approach things differently. They need to let go of their own preferences and habits and let God mold them to be more compassionate, understanding, and loving.

- *If a church is going to change*…behaviors must change. We can't keep doing the same things and just talk about change. As an idea, change is short-lived. It becomes real only when it's put into action.

- *If a church is going to change*…people must get involved. A church is a group of people, not a building, not paid staff, and not a leadership team.

PRACTICAL STUFF FOR PASTORS:
LEADING CHANGE

People must change in order for the church to change.

As an idea, change is short-lived. It becomes real only when it's put into action.

As people become aware of possible changes and work through their concerns, they will begin to embrace the changes. As they embrace the changes and become invested in them, they will implement them. As they implement them, they will see results. Then there will likely be a season of maintenance; but rest assured, another new change won't be too far behind.

By Susan Lawrence

HOW TO CHANGE

ANTICIPATING RESPONSES TO CHANGE

In the fall of 2013, our leadership team led our church through "The Shift." It was as ominous as the name suggests.

We wanted to shift our small-group ministry from fellowship groups to mission teams. Imagine messing with a sacred cow like small groups, with their established relationships and comfortable modus operandi. We knew that we would need to anticipate responses to such a big change. In hindsight, we should have put even more energy into this crucial aspect of leading through change.

Movement Dynamics

Pastors who lead change need to know patterns and trends that help us anticipate how people will react when change is introduced. In order to anticipate responses to change, we need to learn about the dynamics and the players that make a movement happen or not.

Entrepreneur Derek Sivers explains that movements begin like group dancing at a rock concert: they start with a lone nut dancing.[18] This humorous observation can be integrated with Everett Rogers' foundational work on innovation[19] to highlight how church leaders can deal with various responses to change.

- *The change agent or innovator*—a.k.a. "the lone nut": The vision for change is usually born inside one person or a small group of people—no more than 5 percent of the congregation. These visionaries have the ability to see "what could be if…"

  What to expect: If you are the "lone nut," be prepared to share the vision with dogged determination. Naysayers and skeptics will be numerous at this point, so make clear why the change is good, and show how easy it is to follow. Make the change vivid in the hearts and minds of those you hope will follow. Whenever possible, model the desired change.

- *First followers or early adopters*: As the vision is shared, a small group of people—perhaps 10 percent—will say, "Hey, that's a good idea!" They will want to join in the change and by doing so will validate the "lone nut" as a leader. As they share what energized them about the movement, their network of relationships will provide more followers.

  What to expect: First, create an inventory of these people, with their gifts and skills, so you can deploy them throughout the change process. Next, embrace these first followers as equals because they will become another source of leadership. Those who later join the movement will look not to you, but to the early follower(s) who inspired them to join. The spotlight should be on the change, not on the original leader.

At the same time, the original leader must continue to enthusiastically share the vision. It's easy to think the change has succeeded because you've gotten a few enthusiastic people to buy-in.

> The spotlight should be on the change, not on the original leader.

- *Early majority—late majority*: This is what is known as the "tipping point." At some point, the change shifts from a trending groundswell to a movement that makes people feel left out if they aren't participating. Both early and late majority groups will count as about 35 percent of the congregation (70 total). It will be easier to find supporters because the change is socially less risky than it was in earlier stages.

  What to expect: It's tempting for innovators to move on at this point, but if you want the change to set in, your leaders have to develop competencies to lead others through the change. Because the large waves of joiners imitate the first followers more than they do the innovator, it is vital to train the first followers.

- *Church curmudgeons or laggards:* Not everyone will go with the change—maybe 15 to 19 percent.

Some just drift with the flow, some drift away, and others may fiercely fight the current.

What to expect: You may lose some of these people, but some will get noisy. That's okay! Knowing this ahead of time will free you to move on the vision with confidence and wisdom. Don't fight with these people; continue to pastor those who stay, but be relentlessly positive about the vision and change.

Five Tips for Sustainable Change

Anticipating responses to change is not all about negativity. It also focuses on what needs to happen for the change to take root and transform your ministry. Here are five tips to help anticipate what your leaders and people will need in order to sustain the change and keep it moving forward.

People need to know *how* to carry out the change. A pastor...must equip and build expertise in the other leaders.

1. **Build expertise.** Change requires learning new behaviors in uncertain conditions. Business writer and corporate trainer Joseph Grenny says that motivation is important but only half the equation.[20] The other half, which is often overlooked, is the ability side. People need to know *how* to carry out the change. A pastor

serving as change agent must equip and build expertise in the other leaders.

2. **Create a platform to share stories.** When you are casting vision, leading through change, and motivating people to action, they will want to share their successes and what they learned from things that didn't go so well. They will want to be recognized and affirmed. Have them share their stories. Create multiple spaces where that can happen—Sunday mornings, Facebook group, newsletter article, whatever—just give them an outlet.

3. **Continue relentless positive communication.** The most damaging thing to your change initiative will be the back-row whispers and negative side conversations. You can succumb to the negativity, fight against it, and get frustrated, *or* you can counter it with relentless positivity. Step right into those dark whispers and conversations and address the "why" of the change, always focusing on the benefits.

4. **Celebrate the change publicly.** So what do you do with the laggards? You pastor them and engage them relationally, privately, one-on-one. During "The Shift," we didn't demonize the group leaders who wanted their groups to remain fellowship groups. We respected their commitment to their group and their willingness to lead. However, publicly we

shared stories—through social media, sermons, and other platforms—of the groups that *had* shifted to mission teams.

5. **Cultivate a culture of change.** Probably the most effective move you can make to anticipate responses to change is to create a culture where change is expected. Instead of occasional or sporadic change, church leaders can create an environment where change is not even seen as change. The church becomes a laboratory where you adjust in real time in order to meet the needs of people in an ever-changing reality.[21]

Conclusion

We might do well to make a couple of Christ-centered observations to help you confidently lead the change you want to see while anticipating how your people will react.

- Jesus didn't see change primarily as a disruption in the order of things. He saw it as a fulfillment of original purpose (Matthew 5:17). When people question why change is needed, your answer should demonstrate how the proposed change connects to the kingdom of God and fulfills the purpose of the church.

- Jesus implemented change by beginning with a small team of people. Your approach to change will be stronger if it involves a collection of people with various gifts, abilities, and strengths.

- Jesus gave his life to God's mission. If we are leading change in order to better align the church with God's will, it will be a joy to invest ourselves in the process. Being prepared for how people might respond can help change be a truly transformative victory.

"I did not come to abolish the law of Moses or the writings of the prophets. No, I came to accomplish their purpose."

—Matthew 5:17

By Austin Maxheimer

MEASURING EFFECTIVENESS

There is a marked tension around measuring anything in the church. This is understandable. How can you measure the effectiveness of a beloved pastor or youth minister? How can you put a number on spiritual growth and experience of Jesus? It feels so cold and impersonal.

> Measuring the effectiveness of change helps discern if we are good stewards of the resources God has given us.

Yet, if pastors are going to ask people to contribute time, money, and resources to the church's vision, everyone needs to know whether the change is on the right track. And that cannot happen without measuring. We want to appropriately and honorably steward the resources God has given us. Measuring the effectiveness of change helps us discern if we are doing that.

Qualitative Measurement

Here are seven questions you can ask your leadership team to build a bank of qualitative data. These questions assume that the vision for change—the preferred future state—is in place. You will need a large block of time and a blank whiteboard.

- *How often do we have meetings outside the meeting?* Major decisions should be made in the meetings. If major decisions are being made outside the meetings, the vision may be unclear or the team is not fully committed to the change. You may need to go back to clarify and recommit to the vision.

- *How often do we have to revisit decisions?* If the change is effective, you will not have to revisit or second-guess decisions. If this happens frequently, your vision might be shortsighted or in need of further study or revision.

- *Do we have varying points of view, and what is the level of conflict?* If the change is effective, there should be space for healthy but not excessive conflict. If there is no conflict or if there is unhealthy, biting conflict, then the vision was driven by too few leaders with too little support from others. Or people do not feel safe enough to voice a disparate viewpoint. Either extreme is a red flag!

- *How often and what type of questions are people asking?* If the vision is clear and there is a good level of commitment, questions should be focused on activities that support the vision. If questions persist about why the specific vision was chosen, there's not enough clarity or commitment to the vision.

- *Are we solving problems?* If the change is effective, then the problems or challenges we set out to correct are actually being addressed. Look for positive movement toward meeting your objectives.

- *How happy are people here, and how likely are they to recommend us to a friend?* Effective change is contagious. If the word is not spreading on its own, it could be that this change is not inspiring or it hasn't been in place long enough or it is simply not effective.

- *How difficult is it to recruit volunteers?* Change is hard, but when vision is clear and commitment is high, it's not hard to get people to participate. They will know what they are getting into. If you have difficulty recruiting volunteers, look closely at your vision and plans for change.

The answers to these questions should tell you whether enough commitment to the change exists and how broad that commitment is. If that commitment does not exist, you need to go back and get that first.

Now Quantitative Measurement

Once commitment is in place, you can construct meaningful quantitative data that can be used for further accountability. What can and should you put numbers on?

The change you are leading could be anything— ministry philosophy, evangelism efforts, discipleship initiatives, worship style, not to mention the unique dynamics of your church. Therefore, it is difficult to provide a valid quantitative assessment applicable to all churches. Instead, here are two examples of what this might look like.

Move toward intentional discipleship:

- Do the staff members have three conversations per week with potential discipleship leaders?

- Do leaders identify five potential discipleship participants each month?

- How long does it take for a newcomer to enter an intentional discipleship program?

Move toward missional small groups:

- What is the tenure of someone in a missional small group?

- How many missional small-group participants are coming into groups because someone referred them?

- How many missional groups replicate or plant additional groups?

These are things you can actually put a number on. You aren't holding people responsible for the output. They cannot control other people's behaviors or "save" them, but we can (and should) hold them accountable for their input into their ministry. From there, we can measure effectiveness and adjust the change where needed.

Persevere, Kill, Pivot

As your church progresses through the change, use the qualitative and quantitative data you have gathered to guide regular "Persevere/Kill/Pivot" meetings. This will help you discern whether or not you are stewarding change well. Eric Reis, in the book *The Lean Startup*, recommends that less than a few weeks between meetings is too often and more than a few months is too infrequent.[22] You will have to find your own pace.

Persevere: If you know you have high commitment and the metrics indicate your people are taking tangible steps to engage with the change, you have a duty to persevere. It would be irresponsible at this point to make another change or move on to something else.

Kill: Deciding to end something that is not working is not a loss; it is a win. You are saving effort and resources that could instead be focused on what *will* work. It is extremely difficult to make this decision because some people have poured their life into the change. This is why the qualitative and quantitative measurements are so important. They serve as the objective benchmark that cuts through emotional attachments to the plan.

Pivot: This is a third option. Maybe you have high commitment but your activities are not producing the intended outcome. Or maybe an unforeseeable factor arises. It would be irresponsible to kill the change, but neither can you persevere on your current path. A pivot is a "structured course correction designed to test a new

MEASURING EFFECTIVENESS

fundamental hypothesis about the product, strategy, and engine of growth."[23] You must answer the following three questions regarding the change and your pivot:

1. What do we want to achieve?
2. What must be avoided?
3. What can be preserved?

> Qualitative and quantitative measurements serve as objective benchmarks that cut through emotional attachments to ineffective plans.

Conclusion

An important thing to measure in any change is clarity and commitment. If there is clarity about what you are aiming for and sufficient commitment to get there, the battle is mostly won. (Commitment is not necessarily the same as consensus; *I don't have to agree with something to commit to it.*) Many churches don't explore that because it is really hard work. It's much easier to keep doing what you've been doing or work from anecdotal input or emotional reaction. You want to steward well. How can you do that if your people are unclear about the change in the first place?

- On a scale of 0 (no commitment or clarity) to 10 (total clarity and commitment), how would you grade your church or ministry right now?

- What's your plan to ensure there is the right amount of clarity on what is desired so that commitment is achievable?

- What is the potential cost to the church or ministry if you go forward without good clarity or commitment?

- What positive impact might there be if you could go forward knowing that you had clarity and commitment?

When change occurs, we ask people to offer up their money, their precious time, and their lives. Therefore we must be responsible to measure the effectiveness of that process. When we do that, we will be stewarding the change well.

By Austin Maxheimer and Josh Schuler

Endnotes

1. George Barna, *The Power of Vision: Discover and Apply God's Plan for Your Life and Ministry* (Ventura, California: Regal from Gospel Light, 2009), 24.

2. Thom S. Rainer, "Established Churches & Inward Drift," blog, November 26, 2012, http://thomrainer.com/2012/11/26/established_churches_and_inward_drift/.

3. Robert Dale, *To Dream Again: How to Help Your Church Come Alive* (Broadman Press, 1981).

4. These three elements and the Venn diagram are heavily influenced by two books: Rusaw and Swanson, *The Externally Focused Church* (Loveland, CO: Group Publishing, Inc., 2004); Will Mancini, *Church Unique* (San Francisco: Jossey-Bass, 2008).

5. Richard Hooker (1554-1600), British theologian, http://www.brainyquote.com/quotes/quotes/r/richardhoo166260.html.

6. Jean Crawford, "Profiling The Non-Profit Leader Of Tomorrow," Ivey Business Journal (May/June 2010), http://iveybusinessjournal.com/topics/leadership/profiling-the-non-profit-leader-of-tomorrow#.VGGUrsma9jg.